Prophets and Loss

Church Times Study Guide

Prophets and Loss

Exploring the Old Testament

John Holdsworth

CANTERBURY
PRESS
Norwich

© John Holdsworth 2005

First published in 2005 by the Canterbury Press Norwich
(a publishing imprint of Hymns Ancient &
Modern Limited, a registered charity)
St Mary's Works, St Mary's Plain,
Norwich, Norfolk, NR3 3BH

www.scm-canterburypress.co.uk

British Library Cataloguing in Publication data

A catalogue record for this book is available
from the British Library

ISBN 1-85311-685-8
978-185311-685-8

Typeset by Regent Typesetting, London
Printed and bound in Great Britain by Gallpen Colour Print,
Norwich 01603 624893

Contents

Introduction

Choosing a title for any guide to the Old Testament is always a problem. If you include words like 'grappling', or 'wrestling', that seems to suggest that what is involved is some kind of struggle against insuperable odds. If you opt instead for words like 'understanding', or 'accessing', you run the risk of either sounding patronizing or suggesting that what you are about to study is difficult to understand or awkward to access. The sort of thing you might want the title to say, along the lines of 'how to really enjoy the Old Testament a lot more than you ever thought you could, in a pretty short time without having to learn a lot of useless information and confusing jargon', isn't quite snappy enough, and doesn't connect with many people's prior experience and expectation, which is that Old Testament study is more likely to be a duty than a pleasure.

You can understand that, and it's reflected in the kind of things people say when they contemplate doing some Old Testament study.

'It's just so *big* it's daunting. It looks more like an encyclopedia than a book. It's most of the Bible. How can I get a handle on something like that?'

'It's all set in a world I don't have any knowledge of. And in any case when I read the Bible I do that to find out more about life and faith in God nowadays. If I wanted to do a course in ancient cultures I'd enrol for Egyptology.'

'What contact I have had with the Old Testament hasn't been encouraging. There are fantastic stories that actually prove more of an obstacle to faith than anything, or it's totally obscure. In fact the bits that I have understood I've generally found irrelevant.'

If it's any consolation, this study is aimed specifically at people who feel like that. What it aims to do is:

- Describe how scholars themselves have realized that they were making the whole thing far too complicated, and have come to see that perhaps we've been reading the Old Testament in the wrong way for the past couple of hundred years.
- Give someone starting from scratch the kind of overview that will enable them to get a handle on the material, organize it with confidence and read it with pleasure.
- Suggest some of the themes to be found in the Old Testament that really do have a bearing on faith and faith communities today – some of which may even seem more contemporary and recognizable than themes from the New Testament.
- Introduce some of the enormously rich variety of material to be found in this literature.

Exercise

It might be interesting to begin by recalling experiences of the Old Testament so far. Perhaps there are favourite Psalms, or readings from the Nine Lessons and Carols that have proved memorable. Some Bible stories, such as Noah's flood or Jonah and the whale, may be remembered from childhood. It would also be useful to try declaring as a group all the things you most fear about starting on the Old Testament, which may include some of those above. At the end of the study you can revisit the list and see which of them has been put to rest. You should also, then, having read this introduction, be quite robust in listing the things you hope to achieve from the study. Again, you should revisit this list at the end of the study.

Writers, and especially preachers, are often quite timid about sharing the fruits of Bible scholarship for a variety of reasons. I take the view that unless congregation members can really get involved in the business of ordinary theology, church life will remain stunted. It's no use complaining, when some great issue affects the church, that the level of debate is uninformed, if you haven't given people the tools to become informed and to engage in the adventure of theology for themselves. The alternative is patronizing works, which reduce adult congregations to the level of Sunday-school classes and maintain all the power with 'those who know'. This course is an attempt to share, not to talk down.

1

What this Study Will Cover

Time was when studying the Old Testament was of interest only to the kind of people who have name tabs sewn into their underwear and take caravan holidays in the Cotswolds. But suddenly, all that has changed. During the past 20 years or so, the search for ways to make sense of the Old Testament has made this subject perhaps the most interesting, adventurous and exciting field of study in the whole Bible enterprise.

Frequently asked questions (well, they would be frequently asked if people had realized what has happened) include:

1 So what's happened to make this difference?

Basically, three things:

- Shifts in biblical critical methods and philosophies.
- Shifts in our own culture, and the way we organize our knowledge and understand truth.
- New suggestions about how theology should be done.

We shall look at what this means in greater detail in Chapter 2.

2 What new insights has that brought to a subject where just about everything seemed settled, fixed and final?

- The straightforward answer to that, is to say that it has made all those conclusions look a lot more temporary, dated and provisional.

For the more detailed answer look at Chapter 3.

3 What difference does this academic and scholarly study of the Old Testament make to people of faith, and people grasping after faith?

The kind of questions that are prompted here are about:

- Do I have options as a reader?
- How can I use the Old Testament as a resource for faith today?
- What contribution can the Old Testament make to the big issues that confront me today?
- What can the Old Testament tell me about what it means to be a member of a faith community today?

And we shall be looking at them in Chapter 4.

Exercise

At this point you might like to make a list of the things you would like to get out of this study. It might include, for example:

- I would like to become interested in something that I haven't been interested in until now.
- I would like to see what possible application the OT could have to faith today.

At the end of the course you should return to the list to see a) whether you still think those are the relevant questions, and b) whether they've been answered in any way. Alternatively you might like to make a list headed 'Why I have never really been interested in the OT', and see at the end if those reasons are still relevant.

2

Is History a Thing of the Past?

How we handed the OT over to 'experts'

About 250 years ago biblical study was faced with a choice. Until that time, those who wanted to know what the Bible was really saying either regarded the text as a true record of fact, or they interpreted it in a literary kind of way by regarding some of its contents as allegories, parables, or constructed illustrations. But with the rise of science and a new emphasis on scientific method, the so-called modern period was born, academic life boomed, and a new way of determining truth was established. Evidence and reason were the prized commodities now, and there was a danger that the one-time premiership champion, theology, was going to be relegated to a regional league. If it were to hold its own in the academy, it would have to submit to a new set of critical enquiries. Two options were available. Either biblical documents could be studied using the critical tools available to the historian; or they could be studied using the critical tools available to the student of literature. They chose history, and the rest is, well, history.

If you study biblical texts (and for our purposes we shall concentrate on Old Testament texts) using the critical tools available to historians, then these are the assumptions (knowingly or unknowingly) you are making.

- Objectivity is the prime virtue. Scholarship of this kind works on the basis that any rational person, faced with a particular set of evidence, will reach particular conclusions and may argue for them with confidence on the basis of the evidence.

- Historians are interested first and foremost in 'what really happened'. This approach builds into OT study the assumption that what we are interested in is events in the past, and what they meant.
- So when historians study documents from the past they are particularly interested in originality. They want always to get further back. They're not satisfied with a second edition – they want to discover the original. Then they want to know what its sources were, and how or by what process they combined to produce the document in question.
- Underlying this is the assumption that truth is to be discovered through knowing what the document meant in its original setting.
- A further assumption is that there is in fact one truth to be discovered – one right answer to the question 'What does this mean?' – and one way of finding it.
- The text is therefore a means to an end. It is a way of entering the world of the past.
- As a means to an end, the text is thought to be only as interesting as the context from which it supposedly came. So if we read books from the Prophets section of the Old Testament such as Amos, we become interested in the character of the man Amos. We want to find out as much as we can about him, concentrating particularly on passages such as Amos 7.10–17, which gives us apparently biographical information.
- Another assumption is that in order to find out what any part of the OT actually means you need experts. Faced with a passage from, say, 1 Kings, you need someone who knows about these things to explain the historical, social and political background of the supposed events in question. You also need someone to tell you about how the text you are reading actually came into being. That is your only route to know fully what the passage means. And so there opens up the potential for a rift between the academy and the Church, with the former scoffing at the uninformed and primitive naive views of the latter. At its worst, this can turn into a kind of battle between the academy and the Church over the 'ownership' of the text.

Had we lost the plot?

From the eighteenth century almost to the end of the twentieth century, these were the ground rules of biblical study and exegesis (or explanation and application). OT studies became little more than a room on the corridor marked 'historical and anthropological studies'. During the twentieth century, some scholars became more and more concerned about this. One of them, an OT scholar from Germany called Walter Eichrodt, drew attention to it by starting a whole new way of setting out what he thought the OT meant. His concerns were:

- That this historical method was breaking up the text into so many small units that the big picture was being lost.
- That the Judaeo-Christian inheritance, studied as just one of many ancient religions, was in danger of losing its distinctiveness.
- That the kind of studies that were emerging did no justice to the profundity and significance of the material.
- That the link between the OT and the NT was inadequately covered.
- That we knew a lot about ancient religious practice, but not a lot about faith in God.

And so he wrote an 'OT theology', the first of its kind, and began a process that would continue throughout the twentieth century (*Theology of the Old Testament*, SCM Press, 1979). But his attempt was still based on the assumptions of historical method.

About 25 years ago a further significant change took place. Some scholars decided to take route two: studying the Old Testament using the methods available to students of literature. The result is that essentially you hold a completely different set of assumptions. They are:

- There is not just one truth and one way of finding it. There are in fact many truths. Different members of the audience at a Shakespeare play may each take from a performance a different meaning, which may in turn be determined by all kinds of things going on in those people's lives, or be prompted by the director's interpretation.

- It may be that the original author did not foresee or intend some of these 'truths', some of these 'meanings'. There is a sense in great literature that their truth transcends the origins and intentions of the work.
- The meaning of literature has little to do with what happened originally. It has everything to do with 'what it does to you now'. So objectivity is no longer prized; rather, subjectivity is.
- There is little interest in the process of composition. The final version is all-important.
- The text is not a means to an end. It is an end in itself.
- You don't need experts in order to be fundamentally affected by a piece of literature. You can simply enjoy it. And, of course, questions about ownership of the text do not arise. No one can be a gate-keeper to the truth. No one can make salvation copyright.

Exercise

Read Joshua 7. Imagine this, first, as an account of something that really happened and is simply being reported. What problems does that pose?

- For example: what does it mean in verse 10 to say that God answered Joshua? How did he do that? Are we being asked to suspend our normal critical faculties here?
- Also, put yourself in the shoes of Achan. He has done wrong. He admits his guilt fairly readily. Joshua speaks to him quite kindly and encouragingly, and the next thing you know he's being brutally killed, in a scene more like something from *The Godfather* than God the Father.
- Then again, what does it say about God that he demands all this, and even worse, that he's satisfied by it? Could you easily believe in such a God?

If we regard this account as literature rather than history, we can be less concerned by these things, and we can begin to notice other things, such as the way the author intertwines events with 'the lesson' that is to be drawn from them. We can ask new questions about the author's agenda, and also appreciate more fully the storyteller's art in the passage.

How was it for you?

The effect on scholarship has been to give a sense of liberation, new permissions and new possibility. That is not to say that historical method has been abandoned, and many scholars would favour some combination of the two, but it has led to daring new hypotheses, as we shall see. For example, once you think of the text as a literary piece, you begin to think about why it was written. What was the agenda behind it? What point of view was being put across? What techniques are employed to get us to see things in a certain way? In particular, you can ask, in whose interest was this written? Whose voice am I hearing here? And, perhaps even more important, whose voice is being suppressed here? History is normally recounted very differently by the winners and the losers. So in the OT, where is the voice of women, for example?

Exercise

Read 1 Samuel 18. What do you think the author wants the reader to believe? What techniques does he use to make us sympathize with one man rather than the other? Think of this as a kind of newspaper account written by those who support David. Imagine now that there's a paper called 'The Sun: the paper that supports our Saul'. How differently would its account read?

What is truth?

This shift in biblical critical method has coincided with a cultural shift from the 'modern' culture to the 'postmodern' culture. This is a very complicated and multi-faceted phenomenon, but for our purposes the most obvious consequences are to do with truth. The modern age was built on a belief that the world was in effect one system, held together by one big story, and that all truths were connected to one big truth. The postmodern belief is that there are many truths, and many small, relatively unconnected systems and networks that do not depend on one overarching notion of truth. What is true for me is what counts. Clearly there is common ground between this kind of approach to truth, and that of literary scholars, and the coincidence of these two shifts has given even greater impetus to a more subjective approach to OT studies. For critics, this is precisely the weakness. If a text can mean anything you want it to mean, how can you have a standard of truth, and what sense does it make to speak of one divine truth? We shall return to this later.

What is theology?

The final shift is less dramatic, but for a certain kind of OT reader is equally important, and is connected to the other two. That is the shift away from systematic and dogmatic theology, and towards practical or pastoral theology. This mode of theology sees what is essential about theology not as a set of axioms or a system of beliefs, but rather as what happens when religious traditions are applied in a particular context. The practice of theological reflection is important here. That involves bringing together religious traditions, such as the Bible, and contexts in life here and now, in such a way that each has the capacity to transform the other. The effect of this on biblical studies has been a demand to read texts in a way that renders them capable of application in such a process. That is, they have to be useful. They cannot be studied just in the abstract. They must be studied with a view to their application.

These three movements have led us to ask completely new questions of the text, and to reach new conclusions about its meaning. It may be that 3,000 years on, we still haven't actually learned how to read the thing properly.

3

Getting a Handle

Handle 1: It's all about the Exodus

During most of the twentieth century it has been usual to see the Exodus as the theological linchpin of the OT. The Exodus is a shorthand term for the biblical account of how an enslaved Hebrew people escaped their captors in Egypt and were led across Sinai to a promised land, Israel. This they captured from other indigenous tribes, and eventually settled. We read about this in the OT books from Exodus through to Judges. On either side of this linchpin we have events that put it in context. Before it, we have a prehistory of the Hebrew people leading back to an ancestor Abraham (meaning father of a people) contained in the book of Genesis; and after it we have an account of how the people of Israel developed a civilization, and then threw it all away. We read about this in the books of Samuel and Kings. The story fizzles out after the Israelites first become divided into two minor states, and then become exiles in foreign lands. There is a brief postscript, when some of them are allowed to return and begin again, though this part of the story is full of tragic irony and a sense that the great days are over. Books like Nehemiah and Ezra tell of this time. Along the way we have a commentary on some of the events after the land is settled from people called prophets. Originally these are bands of court-related yes-men who operate like professional consultants. Later we see named individual prophets who are profoundly and bravely counter-cultural, and who feel a vocation to speak words of warning and encouragement in the name of the Lord.

The central story of the Exodus is contained in the book of that name and the three following books; and the continuing account of the conquest and settlement is to be found in the books of Joshua and Judges. Within those accounts we find some of the great theological themes of the Judaeo-Christian tradition. We see:

- A God who acts.
- A God who promises and delivers on his promise.
- A God who can form relationships with individuals and nations and who has the grace to do so.

The concrete evidence of this relationship is the covenant made at Sinai, which includes the Ten Words (or commandments, or commitments, depending on whose translation and interpretation you're reading). The terms of this agreement are set out in Exodus 20 and the following chapters. It is this covenant that plays such an important part in subsequent events, as the people are judged by its standards, and punished for failing to keep their side of the bargain. The religious concepts of gift, vocation, service, celebration, sacrifice, sin and judgement are all rehearsed here.

There is a certain logic in reading the OT in this way, and, indeed, that appears to be how we are being urged to read it. Historical criticism had discovered a degree of arrangement and management in the way the texts were presented. It was learned, for example, that the first five books of the OT contain four different sources, the earliest of which dates possibly to the time when Israel was governed by a king (the period of the monarchy), and the latest to the time after the Exile in the sixth century or later. The inter-relationship of these sources is fairly sophisticated. Genesis 1 belongs to the latest source, for example, whereas Genesis 2.4ff belongs to the earliest.

Exercise

Read Genesis 1—2.3. Then read Genesis 2.4ff. These are two different accounts of creation separated by some 400 or 500 years. You might like to explore some of the differences in these two texts by asking questions such as: Which of the two accounts would be more attractive to a member of the Green Party and why? Imagine that each of the accounts was written by a single author. What do you think each would be like? Which of the accounts would make the best children's story? Which would sound better read in public? What is the place of humankind in each account? How do the styles differ? Which one tells a story and which one looks more like a piece of liturgy?

Problems

This kind of approach to the OT invites questions about the historical circumstances of the Exodus. So, school texts contain all kinds of helpful suggestions about possible routes through the Sinai desert, and explanations for the seemingly miraculous crossing of the Red (or should it be Reed) Sea. The traditions are so confused that this is no easy task.

Difficult for other reasons is the account of the conquest and settlement. On ethical grounds, scholars began to be uneasy about the kind of God who could sanction genocide on a whim. The contemporary history of Israel prompted other disquiet about claims of ownership on the grounds that God had decreed it, in the face of other more usual claims to land. Also, archaeological evidence failed to support the account of the conquest and settlement as set out in the first six books of the OT. Some scholars continued to hold the traditional line. Others favoured a view that there was a gradual infiltration into the land of Canaan, and that the freed ex-slaves teamed up with other disaffected natives in a kind of peasants' revolt against oppressive Canaanite overlords. This theory puts God on the side of the good guys, but is contested. Others see no decisive revolt as such, but believe there was a process of peaceful infiltration with occasional skirmishes. In its most extreme view, the conclusion is that the biblical account of the Exodus is not a factual account at all. The facts might be that a few slaves from Egypt brought with them to Canaan the story of a liberator God, and they banded together on socio-economic grounds with indigenous Canaanites, taking the name Israel to describe the new and ultimately victorious entity. Clearly, if your reading strategy for the OT depends upon its being a reliable account of what really happened, such conclusions are fatally threatening. But beyond that, the question is raised as to why these accounts are in fact written in this way. For the past 30 years or so, many scholars have found the answer by looking not at the Exodus, but at the Exile.

The key to this approach is asking questions about the final form of the OT books, and particularly, when and why they were published. And it has become clear that although they may depend upon much more ancient sources, each of the OT books reached its final form after the Exile. The further conclusion is that the demands and challenges of those times set the agenda for the publishers.

In the early 1970s, a disarmingly brief book by David Clines (*The Theme of the Pentateuch*, Continuum, 1996) attempted to find a theme in the Pentateuch, the first five books of the OT. These form the first section of the Hebrew Bible and there is a consensus that these five books belong together. The historical approach had identified lots of theological themes contained within them, as we saw above. Clines, using a more literary based technique, wanted to see if there was one overarching theme that ran through the books, that could be said to be 'what they were about'. He found the theme of partially fulfilled/partially unfulfilled promise to be at the heart of this collection, which initially seems a rather strange conclusion. However, it begins to make sense if we think of the collection's reaching its published form just after the Exile, at a point where some of the exiled are about to return to the promised land and, in effect, enter it for a second time. The issue, or agenda, driving the publication can then be seen as a determination to avoid the fate of those who entered the first time. In other words, it can be seen as a determination to make sense of the experience of Exile and to learn lessons from it.

Exercise

Read Deuteronomy 34. How satisfactory an ending would you find this to a novel whose main theme had been that the people had been promised a land of their own, a special relationship with God and lots of descendants? What would provide a better ending? Now read on, and see how convinced you are by the arguments below.

Handle 2: The Exile

From this kind of study, there grew a new interest in the Exile itself, and particularly in the effect it would have had on the faith of the people of Israel, and their view of God. Essentially, it would have eaten away at the very foundations of their faith. They had been promised a land, progeny and a special relationship with God. Instead they had been taken forcibly from their land, the future of their race was in grave doubt and God appeared to have done nothing to save them. This was a massive crisis for faith, comparable perhaps in some ways with the crucifixion in the NT. The remarkable thing is that in both instances, at the very point where you might expect everyone to give up and religion to die, it actually experienced a huge burst of creative energy and spawned the very publishing enterprises that led to both the OT and the NT.

And so a new way of describing the creation of the OT emerged, not just in terms of sources, but in terms of theological motivation, with the experience of Exile at its heart. It goes something like this.

• When the trauma of Exile first happened, as in any traumatic situation, people asked, 'Why has God allowed this to happen?' One school of writers came up with the answer: it's all the people's fault, and a particular responsibility rests on the king and the leaders. Failure to keep the covenant properly has resulted in this punishment. Those writers produced an account of history to support their idea, and are responsible for the books from Deuteronomy through to 2 Kings in modern Bibles.

Other contemporary voices were at one with this assessment, and they included a number of the prophets, including Jeremiah.

- In Exile, a subtle shift took place. After all, the experience lasted for about 60 years, which meant that a couple of generations had been born who knew nothing of the land of Israel. The shift was from the breast-beating 'it's all our fault' response to the question, 'How could God let this happen to us of all people?' to a new question and a new response. The new question was, 'How shall we survive as a distinctive people of faith in the future?' and the new answers began to present a more optimistic view of the future. Parts of Isaiah and Ezekiel represent this view.

- As the prospect of a return increased, so there was more serious consideration of what had been learned about God in this experience. The people had entered exile with a view of Yahweh, their god, as relatively local. Although the best god, he was, nevertheless, one among many. Now there was a sense that he was with them even in a foreign land, and that he could actually influence events of history in that place. So there grew the idea that Yahweh was the one God. If that were so, he was God of all creation, God of all history, and God of all peoples. Books like Proverbs, Daniel and Ruth respectively are attempts to explore the implications of this.

- If there were to be a return, then the account of the foundation of Israel provided by the existing history was clearly inadequate to make sense of the new situation. A new history was needed that was written not in answer to the question 'Why did this happen?' but rather in answer to the question 'How can we survive from here on?' That history was produced as 1 and 2 Chronicles.

Exercise

Read 2 Samuel 10.19—12.31 and 1 Chronicles 19.19—20.3. These are the different histories' accounts of the same period in David's life. First of all, note the differences. You might like to ask which newspaper would be most likely to carry each account (*Sun, Telegraph,* etc.). If you were David's PR secretary which account would you prefer? What do you think each writer wants us to believe about David? Is the apparently more damaging story a bad press? One explanation is that the Samuel passage is written to show how corrupt the leaders were, as part of the explanation for Exile. The Chronicles passage is written to bolster confidence in the institutions of Israel, which might form part of a survival strategy after the Exile. Do you find this convincing?

These are just a few examples of the new way of describing the OT that has emerged. In a nutshell, this handle would say the OT is a way of coming to terms with the trauma of apparently being abandoned by God, by those who want to retain faith in God. It is an attempt to reflect on the experience of Exile by telling a story about an Exodus.

Scholarly battle lines

There remains an argument about what might be 'salvaged' from the accounts in the Pentateuch in terms of their pointing to 'what really happened'. A vigorous debate is in progress between those who believe that quite a lot can be learned, and that some ancient sources are revelatory, socially and historically; and those who believe, in effect, that most of the material is a fanciful post-exilic creation or fiction. The latter would say that the historical Israel cannot be reached by means of the biblical Israel, and that the confusion of the two has led to catastrophic results, not only in biblical scholarship but also in real life politics. The title of one contribution to the debate, *The Invention of Ancient Israel: The Silencing of Palestinian History* (Keith Whitelam, Routledge, 1996), makes the point.

4

What Difference Does it Make?

The implications of these developments in OT study show that they are not limited to those whose claim to their land is based on a particular reading of the texts. They give everyone a new set of options, permissions and possibilities. They enable a new playfulness, a new imaginative approach with regard to the texts. The reader can now approach them as would a theatre director to a text of *Hamlet* or *King Lear*, and ask, 'How can I relate this to contemporary experience?' They will not be restricted to just one meaning, determined at the time of writing, but informed by a deep appreciation of the emotions and psychology that prompted the work. Here are some examples.

Practical example 1: What kind of social chaos?

 Read Psalm 55.

Imagine this as written by an individual of faith. Clearly something has happened to this person. Without looking at any other commentary or notes, try to imagine the person who wrote this and their circumstances. Which of the following suggestions do you find nearest to your conclusions?

- The lament of a Judean king, which he uttered repeatedly in the Temple against a background of disorder in Jerusalem (J. H. Eaton).
- A lament over social chaos (J. Mays).

- The lament of a woman who has been raped (J. D. Pleins).
- Prayer after having been slandered (New Jerusalem Bible).

Which come closest to your own thinking? Have any of these suggestions helped you think again? Does it make any difference to the importance or relevance of the Psalm for you to adopt a particular setting for it in your own mind? Does this have anything to do with your own experience?

Practical example 2: Setting boundaries and dealing with difference

 Read Genesis 10, and then read 11.1–9.

These two accounts come from different sources. The Babel story is the older, pre-exilic source, and it concludes that difference and diversity are a curse or punishment. On the other hand the genealogy, picking up the command to 'be fruitful and increase and fill the earth' (Genesis 1.28), presents difference and diversity as part of God's plan in creation. In what current issues do you see this debate reflected? You might think about:

- Immigration policy
- Gay and lesbian rights
- Membership of the EU
- Ecumenical co-operation in churches.

What do you conclude from seeing that these two views are placed side by side in the OT? Does it help to know that one is pre-Exile and the other post-Exile? What more do you think you might want to know to be able to use these texts to help reflect on the issues?

Practical example 3: Feeling God-forsaken

 Read Lamentations 2.

This is an anguished poem describing the deep psychological scars of Exile. Are there any ways in which you can identify with these feelings – perhaps as a result of some personal tragedy or bereavement? The new emphasis on Exile has given some writers stimulus to reflect on the texts in a more robust way, that does not always seek to explain or justify God. Here is a recent contribution of that kind, from a chapter entitled 'The Abusing God'.

Although God never speaks directly in Lamentations, the book is highly theological. Four of its five poems speak to God, and all five have something to say about God. The speakers rarely attempt to appease God and they do not spare God. Although they offer contradictory testimonies, the predominant opinion among them is that God is cruel and violently abusive. Lamentations' speech about an absent, abusing God is a blessing, an unnerving but refreshing iconoclasm. It smashes images of a God harnessed to our bidding. It disrupts theologies of a God who makes us prosper in all things, rescues us from every evil, and longs always to be with us. By insisting on honest testimony from the midst of pain, the book takes us to that place of impasse that purges and burns away pseudo-spiritualities and God-diminishing pieties. It invites us into vulnerability where God can be met in what Christians call the Paschal Mystery.
(Kathleen M. O'Connor, *Lamentations and the Tears of the World*, Orbis Books, 2002)

Do you feel that this is a 'blessing'? Do you have any feeling that the OT is somehow more 'grown-up' and contemporary than you might otherwise have thought it?

The OT adventure

Before passing to the next examples you might like to take part in a short experiment. Simply mark each of the following statements on a scale of 1 to 5, where 1 means 'not true at all', and 5 means 'very true'.

Before I started on this course, when I thought of what the OT contained I thought of:

1 Laws
2 Rituals
3 Psalms
4 Nine Lessons and Carols
5 The garden of Eden
6 Cutting edge commentary on how to cope with feelings of abandonment and god-forsakenness
7 Meaningful reflection on questions around suffering and trauma
8 Useful contributions to an understanding of how a faith community might operate nowadays.

My guess is that your list will start with 5s and end with 1s. In a nutshell, the effect of scholarship during the past 30 years has been to enable you to virtually reverse that understanding. That, of course, has implications for how we use the OT in current problem-solving, particularly in regard to laws. To take one contemporary example, how useful is the book of Leviticus in helping us to reach a judgement about the place of gay and lesbian people in churches?

Those who approach this question from the perspective of historical study will say that you must understand the original context of texts such as Leviticus 18.22 and 20.13. The injunctions in these passages are addressed exclusively to men, they are not concerned with sexuality as such but primarily with anal penetration, and they have nothing to say about 'relationships', which is a more modern concern. Moreover they bear witness to social mores, which, though frowned upon, are not now thought worthy of death in Christian cultures, such as adultery, or intercourse with a menstruating woman. In other words, it is false to read from their situation to ours, which is completely different.

The newer studies build on rather than replace those arguments. The authors of Leviticus are among the last contributors to the OT, who have redefined religious life in a far more sacramental way, which has less interest in politics and far more interest in the interconnectedness and sacredness of all creation; a way that is more pacifist, more humble and more green. All of that has come from mature reflection on experiences of Exile. As part of that understanding, the authors see sin very much in terms of upsetting the balances and connections of this creation through defilement and anything that could be called unnatural. This theological understanding gives a different context for understanding the words. Beyond that, however, there is now debate about whether these laws (which are part of something called the Holiness Code) were ever put into effect, or whether, rather, they were just aspirations and illustrations. If the latter, it might be more in line with the intention of the authors if we were to see environmental pollution, smoking and economic exploitation as examples of that theology.

These are just a few examples of the difference that a new approach to OT study can make in terms of contemporary issues and experience. There is a lot at stake in terms of:

- How we understand God.
- How we understand the inspiration of scripture.
- The importance we place on historical events as foundations of our faith.
- How we use scripture in our church and in our lives.

It has a bearing, also, on how exciting, how relevant, how inspirational the OT can be in terms of our mission. Tomorrow's readers have all but abandoned the caravan in the Cotswolds. When they're not skiing in the Alps they're enjoying their timeshare in Gran Canaria. And no, they don't have name tabs.

5

What to Do Next

If you would like to continue with study of the Old Testament, here is some of the available material.

You might like to read or buy a handbook to the Old Testament. Probably the best known and widest used is John Drane's *Introducing the Old Testament* (Lion, 1987). Handbooks contain a wealth of historical, geographical and cultural material that is interesting in its own right. They also contain what are usually uncritical introductions to the text, as related to that background material.

You might like to read or buy an introduction to the Old Testament that takes account of the kind of scholarship outlined in this guide. Introductions take three forms. Some introduce the individual books of the Old Testament; some introduce the themes, ideas and history of studying the Old Testament; and some attempt to do both. It is probably best to start with either of the latter two categories. My *SCM Studyguide to the Old Testament* (SCM, 2005) has both a 'how to read' section, and an introduction to individual books and genres in what aims to be a very accessible way. *The Original Story* by John Barton and Julia Bowden (DLT, 2004) covers similar ground and has quite an involved series of reader helps. Of the other kind of introduction, I have generally found Richard Coggins' *Introducing the Old Testament* (OUP, 1990) particularly good.

More thematic studies you might find interesting and readable include Richard Friedman's *Who Wrote the Bible?* (HarperCollins, 2nd edn, 1997); and David Clines' *The Theme of the Pentateuch*, referred to above.

Or you may simply (having whetted your appetite) want to look forward to the next *Church Times* Study Guide.